We
Were
Once Here

We
Were
Once Here

Michael McFee

Carnegie Mellon University Press
Pittsburgh 2017

Acknowledgments

Thanks to the editors of these periodicals for first publishing these poems:

Appalachian Journal: "Dew Rot," "Crick," "Scattered." *Chapter & Verse*: "The First." *The Cincinnati Review*: "Dust to Dust," "Frosted Windows in a Small-Town Presbyterian Church." *Crazyhorse*: "High Cross." *Hudson Review*: "Fingal's Cave," "The Roentgens." *Inch*: "Scan, Stage 4," "*Oh god*," "Buried." *Nantahala Review*: "Roadside Table." *News & Observer, Sunday Reader*: "Fats Waller." *Ploughshares*: "Yardsticks." *River Styx*: "Ovation," "Sweet Chariot Car Wash." *Shenandoah*: "Breaks." *Southern Cultures*: "Cast-Iron Ghazal." *Southern Poetry Review*: "Snoring," "Beige Wall Telephone, 1960s," "There, There." *The Southern Review*: "*I swan*," "Straw Poll," "Sunday Paper." *Stone Canoe*: "Cremation." *Tar River Poetry*: "Burn." *The Threepenny Review*: "The Death of Randall Jarrell."

Some of these poems were reprinted as follows: "Ovation" in *American Life in Poetry*; "Roadside Table" in *Edible Piedmont* and in *Cornbread Nation 3: Foods of the Mountain South*; and "Snoring" and "Beige Wall Telephone, 1960s" in *Poetry Daily*. "The Massage" appeared in *Intimacy: An Anthology*, and "Loggerhead Hatchling" appeared in *Southern Poetry Anthology, Volume VII: North Carolina*. *Hard Lines: Rough South Poetry* featured "Yaller." "Beggar's Lice" was featured in *FLOW: An Exhibition at the Hillsborough Gallery of Arts*.

The epigraph to Section I is a one-line poem, "Appalachia," from *The Smallest Talk*, Bull City Press, 2007.

Thanks to the following, at UNC-Chapel Hill, for support which made it possible for me to research, write, and revise some of the work in this book: the Women's Leadership Council, for a Faculty Mentoring Award; the College of Arts and Sciences, for a W. N. Reynolds Research and Scholarly Leave; and the Department of English and Comparative Literature, for a Research and Study Assignment.

And finally, thanks to Michael Chitwood, my fellow mountaineer, whose feedback over the decades has been more helpful than I can ever say.

Book design by Connie Amoroso

for Philip Pickett McFee

Contents

1.

11   *I swan*

12   Dew Rot

14   Cast-Iron Ghazal

16   Crick

17   Snoring

19   Burn

20   Roadside Table

22   Yardsticks

24   Beige Wall Telephone, 1960s

26   Straw Poll

27   Breaks

29   Yaller

31   Ambeer

32   Dead Man's Pinch

33   *The North Carolina Gazetteer*

2.

37   Ashen

38   Scan: Stage 4

39   *Metastasis*

40   The Day of Her Diagnosis

41   Radiation

42   Quiet Room

43   O_2

44   Palliative

45   The Best

46   Lucky Bible

47   "Stars in Your Crown"

48   *Oh god*
49   Clammy
50   Vigil's End
51   Inboxes
52   Cremation
53   Ashes
54   Scattered
55   Buried
56   Is Love
57   Steam Room

3.

61   Fingal's Cave
65   High Cross
66   Beggar's Lice
67   Loggerhead Hatchling
69   Sunday Paper
70   The First
71   Dust to Dust
72   The Death of Randall Jarrell
73   The Roentgens
77   Frosted Windows in a Small-Town Presbyterian Church
78   Thirst
79   *There, There*
80   Sweet Chariot Car Wash
81   Ovation
82   The Massage
83   Fats Waller

1.

Blue echoes in my speech like hazy ridges

I swan

Instead of "I swear," "I declare," "I vow,"
our mom would say *I swan* when mad or tickled

and sometimes even *I swanny*, that tiny
uplift in the suffix adding another syllable
of astonishment or utter disbelief.

It may be that the phrase came from the Scots
I's warrant ye, "I will guarantee you,"

adopted as a euphemism for "I swear"
and used by Christians to avoid that verb
as Jesus warned in the Sermon on the Mount,

but I doubt that my come-to-town mother
knew or cared about its etymology:

she said *I swanny* because it was something
her fearsome beloved granny had said
when stirred, a pithy subject-verb outburst

that waited in mom's mouth for decades
until she could say it to her own cheeky kids,

reaching without thinking way back
to a shady slope deep in Haywood County
and digging up its potent forked root.

We knew to be still when we heard *I swan*.
We hoped our tears would be tears of laughter.

Dew Rot

Great-aunt Mae told us kids
matter-of-factly
that if we kept going barefoot

outside before
the sun had dried the grass

we'd get dew rot,
summer night's condensate
sneaking its way

into the feet through sole-cracks,
surely leading

to sores or rashes or boils,
our reckless flesh
poisoned by the bitter droplets

we'd foolishly
chosen to run unshod through

without waiting
for the cool wetness to burn off:
though all she said

was *dew rot*, we imagined the rest,
the itch, the ache,

the hobbled agonizing decay
ending in crutches
or oozy bandaged stubs or death,

that wet dark earth
the fate waiting for us all one day.

Cast-Iron Ghazal

My mouth won't ever forget her skill with a skillet,
my father's mother, cooking
with her mother's skillet.

Looking deep into its heavy antique mirror, I see
her wedding day: white dress
and this coal-dark skillet.

Heaven was bacon's sizzle waking my ears and nose.
Or was it one of her chickens
slow-frying in the skillet?

Her husband once took it hunting without asking:
she said she'd bust his skull
with that upraised skillet.

Fire-born bell whose clapper was a plain dinner fork,
juicy fauna and flora notes
rang out from her skillet.

I see early widowhood, cooked-for children gone:
darkness lends its seasoning
to every cast-iron skillet.

She hid its teardrop handle inside her strong grip
when pouring red-eye gravy
from one lip of the skillet.

What went into the oven as batter we two mixed
came out as cornbread glory,
steaming amen in a skillet.

Black as her Bible, black as her once-maiden hair,
black as a panther howling
at midnight, this skillet.

I see her funeral day, the kitchen filled with food
not made by her, no flame
kissing the empty skillet.

I say *McFee* into its circle, hear her savory voice
giving back the family name
from her (now my) skillet.

Crick

Granny always woke up
with one in her thin neck
no matter what pillows
she used or how she slept,

as if an underground
creek flowed up her spine
and froze every night
at the higher elevations,

that elemental cramp
thawing as the day warmed
and her head, unlocked,
resumed its hawklike watch.

Snoring

With toil of breath. —Coleridge

My father, who loved the comics, became Dagwood
every night: "SKNX-X-X-X" his open sleeping mouth

would utter, part of an untranslatable somniloquy

I'd hear through the flimsy wall between his twin bed
and mine, my dad a rackety wee-hours mockingbird

doing chainsaw, hog call, flooded car, horse snort,

snout and throat and cheek and trembling soft palate
shaping his respiration into an improvisation

that would sometimes suddenly simply halt, cut off

mid-phrase as if strangled into the deadest silence,
and my mother and I would wonder if this was it,

maybe he'd pushed his virtuoso breath beyond

the outer blackout limits of mortal endurance,
maybe he'd snorkled too deep and couldn't quite

make it to the surface without choking on water,

though just as I was about to pound on the wall
or she was rising to cry, "Bill!" and run to his bed

he'd exhale, rejoining the living breathing world,

sometimes relaxing into a snoring so sotto voce
it finally lulled us to sleep, a tender lip-puffing

almost like he was blowing us faint farewell kisses,

a mellow interlude before the next thunderstorm
of snores he'd pour on our heads until morning,

gargling the house's gloom then broadcasting it

in hiss and bleat and gag and growl and snuffle,
never hearing his guttural proto-language

whose slapstick consonants refused to settle down.

Burn

Our old man wore white socks
twice during summer vacation,

the first afternoon on the beach
with loafers and no sunscreen,

thereafter with no shoes at all,
bright pink legs cooled with aloe,

bare lower calf and ankle and foot
pale as a corpse's below the sockline,

that bleached stocking of flesh
the dazzling negative of *burn*.

Roadside Table

It was an ugly slab of rough concrete

or warped green boards carved and stained
by greasy sticky previous picnickers

but still we'd pack the creaking station wagon

with hungry relatives and cardboard boxes
full of deviled egg luster under wax paper

and fried chicken's golden warm aroma

and the sweet strata of granny's coconut cake
before dad drove for what felt like forever

until he saw a blue sign for one just ahead

and pulled off into a shady dirt turnout
between the busy highway and some river

where we all waited while meticulous aunts

brushed off the crumby weathered surfaces
and unfolded a tablecloth of newspapers

held down with the cooled unloaded feast,

starving, suffering through interminable grace
then loading our flimsy plates with layers

of food as if we never ate at home,

as if we didn't have our own picnic table
around which, anytime, everyone could gather.

Tourists driving by us might have laughed

at this simple mountain clan that had to eat
at a borrowed wayside table, too dirt poor

to afford an inside dining room of their own,

just as shoulder-walkers were to be pitied
for not having enough money to own a car,

but they'd have been wrong: it was pure holiday

to linger in that place, in public privacy
between the currents of road and water,

cooled by the luxurious breezes of both

as cousins skipped flat rocks to the far bank
or waded on shivering legs into the river

and cigarette smoke rose toward the understory

and the ripening barrels hummed electric with bees
and watermelon seeds shone blackly under the laurels.

Yardsticks

Skinny printed boards
half ad, half measurement,
they came home with dad
from businesses he visited,
their names and numbers
and *Lowest Prices!* slogans
branded into cheap wood
like on giveaway pencils.
Lightweight, I'd wield one
as a club, a sword, a bat:
if it splintered, no problem,
there were plenty of trees
and we could find more,
it was like taking toothpicks
when leaving a restaurant.
Three times the foot-length
of any gradeschool ruler,
they helped mom measure
her two kids' progress up
the kitchen door's jamb,
our time-lapse marathon
to an overhead finish line,
each height noted in pencil
at semi-annual intervals:
at first I was a fraction taller
than the thirty-six wooden inches
from some furniture store,
and beanpole older sister
towered over little brother,
but years later I passed her

during a teen growth spurt.
Then the markings stopped.
I'm the last one vertical:
they lie side by side by side
two dark yardsticks down
in the hilltop graveyard.

Beige Wall Telephone, 1960s

To you who have never known what it is to be tethered
    to the family's one phone by a corkscrew cord
        filthied by idle fingers twisting it as we talked
and stretched by our efforts to sneak with the handset

away from the dining room where that cheap plastic box
    clung to the wall, my sister and I desperate
        to hide behind curtains or in a nearby room
and mumble dumb endearments to whichever lucky soul

we had a crush on that week: I won't say how wonderful
    it felt to hear a call's unexpected tremolo
        and rush to answer that sudden summons,
yanking the receiver's heavy curve up out of its cradle,

or to dial seven numbers on a whirring analog wheel
    and hear a distant ringing pulse in the ear,
        knowing that actual bells trilled as a body
moved through space to deliver its hopeful *Hello?*—

no, it was awful, that phone, intended for businesses,
    brisk standing exchanges of information,
        not a home where its too-public anchoring
left adolescent siblings open to each other's mockery

and the cocked ears of nosy parents straining to decode
    one side of conversations as we curled closer
        to the wall and whispered sounds downward
into the shadow that our huddling made, not pacing

like a barking dog chained to a stake in the backyard
but trying our best to vanish, descending
slow as a diver sipping words like oxygen
from a humming line whose other end kept us breathing.

Straw Poll

I was only 14, but I voted for George Wallace
or at least for his ninth-grade representative
in language arts because—the criteria that day—
his speech and logic were much more persuasive.
Humphrey and Nixon didn't have a chance.

Ted was a future lawyer who, from birth, knew
how to smile or frown or whisper or pause or hold
eye contact with his audience, converted doubters,
and how to spin shitty straw into gleaming gold.
Who knows what he really said? It sounded true.

I can't believe the young me voted for that racist.
I can't believe Ted argued Wallace's case, either,
though maybe it was merely a rhetorical exercise
like debating whether day or night is better.
I can't believe our teacher set up such a contest

but she did, and counted ballots, and, straightening,
simply said, "George Wallace" to her white pupils
in that mountain classroom, in the fall of '68,
when integration was a cloud coming over the hills,
the color of a bruise, about to deliver lightning.

Breaks

Work was something we did between breaks,
those fifteen-minute vacations twice a shift

when everybody stopped stomping the foot pedals
that sent our massive machines into their cycles

of bending or pressing or welding or trimming
the steel pipes that required quick human hands

to position and turn and lift and package them
in that long gone auto parts plant in Arden.

We'd hustle down the narrow concrete aisles
to a low room under the bosses' platform

where the machines we really wanted to touch
were waiting, humming quietly, glowing—

the ones that wouldn't chop or crush our fingers,
the ones that gave us drinks and snacks and smokes

in exchange for the warm coins in our pockets,
the silver circles dirtied by our touch.

Lunch was a longer breather halfway home
when most of us drifted outside to eat,

away from the heat and din and oily stink,
but it was the other breaks that kept us going:

those quarter-hours included our walking time
to and from that official Concession Area,

even if it took seven minutes each way
and left us only sixty frantic seconds

to gulp a coke and choke down a few nabs
and take some puffs on a fresh cigarette

before grinding it out and heading back
to our distant stations in that factory,

fueled for the next few hours of doing
the same job our mindless bodies always did,

resuming the manufacture of tailpipes
designed to fit under machines like the ones

we drove to work that and every other day,
already looking forward to our first break.

Yaller

My stringy step-cousin was a gullet with legs:
he was never not eating
but what he liked best was a mustard sandwich,

two slices of white bread
slathered with yellowest French's, all condiment,
no meat. He'd lick the knife

then slap the halves together and devour it
in quarters, four big bites
followed by four bigger gulps and pained grunting.

Terry smeared Duke's mayo
on the left side "for lubrication," he said the time
I tried one of his sandwiches,

hoping to impress him with my own appetite,
choking before chasing
that dry wad with cold milk whiter than the bread.

He broke my left arm once,
tripping me with a low rope stretched taut across
the top step of our front porch:

he ran away for days, hiding in unlocked garages
until the cops found him
and his dad's belt delivered its familiar lesson.

Years later, Terry killed himself
alone in his car at my sister's house, who knows why,
gun pressed to head, a dull pop

behind rolled-up windows. He was never not doing
something with his hands,
those nailbit hands, those always famished hands

making a "yaller sandwich"
and swiftly taking it into his mouth while standing,
squeezing a little of the filling

around his bulging lips, that sour gold bright
as a road's double center line
or signs on the shoulder warning trouble ahead.

Ambeer

Cigarette breath was bad enough,
imperceptible exhalations
converted into thin gray bitter exhaust
blown from face to face,
choking every room with smoke,

but what a chaw or pinch of tobacco
did to saliva was worse:
ambeer, too cheerful and pretty a word
for that foul oral liquid,
a stream of sewage-brown spittle

aimed at spittoons or cuspidors
or dribbled into tin cans
children were warned never to tip over,
indoor privies filled daily
by the mouths of ruminating kin

nobody else would ever want to kiss
except another dipper.

Dead Man's Pinch

is what grandmother's spinster sisters
called inexplicable bruises
lurking beneath the surface of our skin,

as if deceased progenitors
came back to squeeze a little warm flesh
between thumb and forefinger

to test our ripeness for the afterlife,
to flirt with the fresh girls
and warn the boys to behave themselves,

to try and wake us up
with that foreshadowing of putrefaction,
its noxious inward eclipse,

leaving their prints on our tender flesh
though we couldn't recall
where or when or how we'd gotten them,

from what cold hard touch.

The North Carolina Gazetteer

My elusive highland forebears
never did get the family surname attached
to knob or ridge or gap or hollow

despite living in the mountains of this state
longer than it's been a state,

couldn't stay in one spot long enough,
or shrewdly enough, or meaningfully enough,
to leave some sign of our presence,

much less our influence,
on spring or branch or pond or fork or river,

as if our clan were an anonymous creek
that dried up before ever making it
to anybody's cartography.

We might as well have stayed put
across the Atlantic, shivering above Ireland

on a wee remote Scottish island
named for a saint, not us,
and let those bloodthirsty McDonalds

slaughter weak McPhees till not a single soul
was left to emigrate to America,

where their rich name glows above highways
and dignifies a mill and a small town
and other Tar Heel places,

where even Shit-Britches Creek
in our native southeast Buncombe County

gets its very own entry: I'd settle
for McFee's Sinkhole, or McFee Mica Mine,
or McFeedon, a ghost village

swallowed up by Pisgah National Forest
or drowned under the power lake,

for the least lost geography whose name
still echoes ours, if only on paper,
reminding the map that we were once here.

2.

Not so much "She has cancer" as "It has her"

Ashen

Opening the front door to my knocking niece—
whom I hadn't seen in a year, the only daughter
of my late sister and a father she never knew—

I almost gasped: her face was grayish, her eyes
tired and deep-shadowed, her shoulders slumped
as if from carrying great weight far too long.

She's really sick, I thought, and helped her inside.
I saw that same ashen color at Mount St. Helens,
miles of dead trees leveled by blast and scorch,

and, in the gift shop, a souvenir bear figurine
made from the ashes collected and compressed
then shaped to resemble an unsuspecting creature

obliterated that mild morning the volcano blew.

Scan: Stage 4

When the cancer came into view, it lit up her right lung

like a big city at night seen from a plane six miles above,
a glowing cluster, soon to spread into the dark countryside.

Metastasis

First used in a medical sense to describe
"the *Metastasis* of the Morbifique matter."

"Morbific," causing disease. That was in 1663.
"Most incorrigible and obstinate *metastases*."

By the time we saw it, the adenocarcinoma
had migrated to her spine (hence the backache),

her adrenals, her brain. Beyond correction:
incorrigible. Adhering stubbornly: obstinate.

"We can't cure you but we can treat you,"
said the doctor, when Stephanie asked him.

Metastasis sounds like a kind of heaven,
a state beyond stasis, a transcendent balance,

though in her case it meant the opposite.
This kind of cancer was once called "terminal,"

though nobody uses that end-word anymore.

The Day of Her Diagnosis

That morning, I took my time getting dressed,
then walked outdoors into fog so dense
I couldn't see anything or anyone

except my own body, its top front half,
the upright chest, the arms swinging, slightly.

That night, I walked out of the clinic
into darkness that felt like fog, metastasizing
to smother everything except the sound

of a soldier playing "Taps," spare, unembellished,
at the VA hospital just up the block.

Radiation

The new cancer center had courtesy valet parking
and a pianist playing at the foot of the open stairwell
and expensive paintings in the clinic's waiting areas

and a state-of-the-art linear-accelerator machine
that targeted high-energy x-ray beams into her skull
for two straight weeks, trying to arrest or shrink

the tumor on the brain, where cancer had spread.
It really hurt—the table, the stifling protective mask—
but she did what they said. Results: inconclusive.

She lost all her hair, except for a tuft on her nape.
She bought some terrible wigs that she rarely wore.

Quiet Room

After she declined chemotherapy, we went to the Quiet Room,
"A Healing Space Designed To Nourish Your Body, Mind, And Spirit."

Everything about it was meant to soothe—the circular walls,
the adjustable light and sound (we chose *sunrise* and *running water*),

the glass table-sculpture in the middle, glowing aqua blue,
the dozen seats around it under a canopy of treelike wooden arches,

the recessed ceiling-circle overhead, its understated radiance—
and I hope it calmed Stephanie in her wheelchair, exhausted and silent.

But I doubt she was nourished, and I know she wasn't healed.
I admired the elaborate in-house production, its concept and ambiance,

though it felt like the set for a futuristic divine council scene
and I couldn't wait to get my unquiet thoughts out of that faux heaven.

O$_2$

After a pulmonary embolism, she was tethered
to the oxygen machine 24/7, its rumble and pulse
filling the house as it spritzed O$_2$ into her nostrils

through the cannula whose plastic tubing hooked
around each ear before slithering to the floor,

trailing behind her like a spacewalker's lifeline
dragged step by weary step across heart pine
into bathroom or bedroom as she closed the door.

The watery gargling of the oxygen condenser
made me feel like a fish, recircling its glassy tank.

Palliative

For months, I would count out her meds into a plastic cup
after breakfast, mid-afternoon, then an hour before bed:

Tylenol Extra Strength, Oxycodone, Oxycontin, Morphine,
Dexamethasone, Gabapentin, Mucinex, Codeine, Senna,
and, eventually, Trazodone, Lorazepam, Haloperidol.

Mornings were hardest, when she needed the most help.
I rattled the pills like a beggar, hoping for a small miracle.

How many thousands of those crisp shapes did she swallow,
their lift and relief vanishing inside her, that brief light
extinguished by a malady no known drug could cast out?

The Best

"Love is the best medicine," said the social worker
at the beginning of her first and last visit to see my niece.

"Everything works out for the best," my niece said
as the woman left, smiling farewell, disinfecting her hands.

No it isn't, I thought. *And no it doesn't*, I wanted to say
to the girl I held in the hospital the cold day she was born,

wishing the best to every cell in that brand-new body.
Who could imagine the doom banked in two mutated genes?

"How are you?" I went in and asked. "Oh, I'm good,"
she said. "And you're the best uncle ever," another placebo lie.

Lucky Bible

She'd never been much for church, or religion,

but once she knew she'd never drive again
and let me clean out her old Jeep, Libby, to sell,

I found a black Bible up under the driver's seat.
"I know it's silly, but it made me feel better,"
she said, then added: "Please leave it there for now."

Did it keep her safe on the road, all those miles
beneath the springs, in that gritty dimness?

I wish God's word had taken fate's bullet for her.

"Stars in Your Crown"

"This will be stars in your crown in heaven,"
the stranger said, hugging me.

What I wish I'd said to her, but didn't, was:
Madam, I don't like crowns,
and even if I thought there was a heaven where

my big head might be crowned,
I don't like the idea of earning celestial jewels

by doing what any human being
should do, taking in his ill and orphaned niece
until she's healed or passed on.

But if you could convert the metastatic lights
from her CT scan into stars

and then affix them to whatever dazzling crown
Stephanie might be wearing
in whatever kind of afterlife she finally reaches

after profoundly unregal agony,
to that I would say: *Amen. Long live the queen.*

Oh god

During her final inarticulate phase, deep grunts and moans
when she shifted or had to be shifted in the bed,

those were the only two words she could manage to say,
Oh god or sometimes *Oh god oh god,* involuntary

utterances arising from unrelieved and unreachable pain,
nothing like ecstasy or prayer, as far as I know.

Clammy

Her nails blued toward the end
and her skin grew colder, colder,
as if she were freezing inside out:

I was prepared for that, and for
the yellow hue her flesh took on,
its jaundiced neonatal tone,

but not for the clamminess
that coated her, a dank sticky pall,
the cold sweat of the nearly dead.

Vigil's End

The night she died, her shallow breath would
quicken now and then, a triple pant

followed by a long unsettling pause (*Is she gone?*)

and, later, an exhale more honk than death rattle,
like the hollow call of a migratory bird

separated from its flock, crossing the high ridge

where her late mamaw's mamaw was waiting,
the ancestor who surfaced in my niece

slipping beyond any grip or reach, an old woman

whose gray chin stubble glistened as she stared
fixedly at something in the distance,

her dried-out mouth agape and, finally, silent.

Inboxes

Once the hospice nurse's fingers could no longer find a pulse,
he checked his watch and gently spoke the time of her death
then phoned the cremation service to come pick up the body.

It would take a while for two men and their van and a gurney
to get to our house, at 2 a.m., so we went to the living room
where he filled out the certificate on his laptop, and I waited,

drained, until he finished, drained, and still no men or van,
so he stretched, and smoothed out his rumpled blue scrubs,
then (nothing else left to say or do) opened his e-mail account

and I did the same, on my own computer, checking messages
as if some good news might finally be brightening our inboxes,
anything to fill the yawning silence and the outer darkness.

Cremation

The "cremation society" was in a small office park north of downtown.

A few of us gathered in the chapel, to talk a little about Stephanie.

Her body lay under a cloth, in its Minimum Alternative Container.

We semicircled our chairs around her, quietly shared some stories.

Two men came and slowly rolled her down the aisle, out of the room.

The funeral director showed us where to stand, along the right wall.

I'd noticed the closed window, assumed it offered an outdoor prospect.

Thick doors on its other side swung back to show the cremation chamber.

My niece waited in her box on a gravity conveyor, its metal rollers still.

I couldn't see the oven to the left, though its glow brightened that room.

The licensed cremation technician wore a padded silvery asbestos suit.

He looked like an extra from a low-budget science fiction movie.

Then he gave a push, and her boat disappeared into the fiery cave.

We kept staring through thermal glass till somebody shut the doors.

Ashes

Her dust, bagged in heavy plastic
with a chrome tag and I.D. number,
filled a rigid cardboard box
labeled with the date of her cremation.

Light gray, it looked like airy powder
but felt gritty and particulate
as concrete mix that's ready to be stirred
with water into everlasting hardness.

Scattered

She wanted her ashes scattered in the mountains
along with those of her mini-dachshunds

so I hauled three boxes up a steep shady trail,
under the blooming rhododendrons and bee-hum.

At the small bluff, after some prayer book words,
I dipped gloved hands into her weighty bag

and tossed pale grayness toward a far ridge:
some clumped and fell straight down, some drifted

neatly into the distance, but some blew back
toward me, onto my gray T-shirt, into my gray hair.

I turned, eyes closed, until the wind shifted,
then quickly scattered what was left to be scattered.

The rock underfoot and leaves below, ash-frosted,
would be cleaned by a late-day thunderstorm.

The mountains looked on, witnesses not mourners,
blue but unmoved, likewise returning to dust.

Buried

With a rusty bulb planter, I dug a hole
between my father and my mother

and buried a silver vial of Stephanie there,

between her grandparents, the place she lived
as a child: now an ounce or so of her

will always be hidden in that Asheville cemetery

with its fine prospect, Pisgah to the south,
the peak of a ridge where one's ashes

might be scattered toward the promised land.

Is Love

What I didn't say, at the memorial my niece said
she didn't want, was: "What will survive of us is love."

That's the only line I could find, in the hundreds
of death and bereavement poems I read after she died,

that sounded almost true: it came from Larkin,
an unlikely source, the last line of a mostly dour poem.

But I liked how he said "will" rather than "may,"
and his use of "survive," how its labiodental v's anchored

the end of "love," a sometimes too-abstract noun
but all that's left now her body is burned, scattered, gone.

Steam Room

Weeks later, in the steam room at the gym,
I think of Stephanie, somewhere else,

and wish I believed there might be a heaven
like this, billows of hot blissful clouds
obscuring her worn-out flesh that suffered

so deeply for so long, down to its genes, now
sweatily and happily forgetting itself.

A father and son on the opposite bench
mumble amiably in tropical fog, in Japanese
or whichever comforting tongue is spoken

in such an afterlife, all walls and bodies erased
by the steam whose steady pulsing breath

is God in Genesis and not the machine
whose oxygen she was moored to for months,
until all she can see is a painless radiance

surrounding and penetrating and melting
everything in this room and inside herself,

including the cancer nothing could stop,
the memory of it a droplet on her bald head,
trickling down rosy skin then disappearing.

3.

Wind stirring the chimes again, earth's breathing belled

Fingal's Cave

Gaelic "Uamh-Binh" ("Cave of Melody")

1.

Otherworldly, or sub-this-worldly,
like a vast fantastic basement
for some centuries-gone castle or cathedral
isolated on the island
of Staffa in the far-flung Hebrides,
this deep towering echoing sea cavern's floor

is the bitter north Atlantic Ocean narrowed
to an almost tropical blueness
that never stops surging
and crashing into the cave, whose far back wall
has a base pink as the rarest marble
or beef, whose sides are clustered hexagonal pillars

glistening dark red as if spritzed with blood
or beet juice, whose ceiling
is a chopped-off basaltic hive patinaed green
by centuries of tides and weather
and humans ferried over from less remote rocks,
exhaling their awed breath upwards.

2.

All people here are tourists, like us,
our cameras and flashes
overmastered by this weirdly sculptural cavity

yet proving *we were there,*
no less than the famous nineteenth-century seekers
of everything sublime and picturesque—

Mendelssohn, whose *Hebrides* overture
with its six-step descending motif
sounds seasick as he'd been on the rough passage,
Keats then Wordsworth then Tennyson
miffed by the vulgar crowds
but praising nature's "Cathedral of the Sea,"

Turner, who painted Staffa as swirling steam,
Queen Victoria and her family
on the royal barge rowed far into the cave,
her men uplifting three loud cheers
before backstroking carefully out
as a solitary bagpiper played "for atmosphere"—

but also earlier pilgrims, including
the naturalist who renamed it "Fingal's Cave"
after an Irish myth, the Vikings
admiring the ruthless power that made this hole,
the stray monks fleeing Iona,
the Druids enacting their solstice sacrifices,

humans who went into this place
and found themselves undeniably stirred
and later tried to convert it
into notes or words or pictures or something
that might make people feel what they felt here,
but failed.

3.

And yet we keep returning to this isle
slightly atilt from a distance—
a three-layer cake fallen at one end,
tuff under massed columns under volcanic debris—
and its cavern whose famed maw
waits for us to come from the ferry landing,

edging across a six-sided-rock causeway
at the base of the basalt cliff
that dwarfs us like a giant's colonnade,
its overhanging billowing gray crown
a troubled cloud looming,
about to break, crushing our eggshell heads,

finally walking under a lofty arch
a little way into the cave of melody, a place
as much air and sound as stone,
its song not the fitful music of our voices
soon fallen silent
but the surging and retreating rise and fall

of the channelled oceanwater below
whose swells are relentless,
whose tide won't cease trying to transform
this long cavern into a tunnel,
to hollow out Staffa and someday collapse it
into the ocean, another legendary ruin . . .

Or is it more like stepping inside a geode
cracked open by the Atlantic,
volcanic lava crystallized then slowly cooled
into prismatic pillars
and colors more peculiar than any lithosphere
we could ever imagine or dream?

"It baffles all description," said Walter Scott.

High Cross

Not symbolic, that ring
circumscribing the crux of Celtic crosses,

not a halo or pagan sun
whose outline circles the intersection
of upright post and shorter transverse piece

like heaven and earth
eternally looped together by God's love,

but structural, practical:
the arms of the massive high crosses
carved and raised well over 1200 years ago

kept shearing off, falling,
too heavy to sustain their widespread span,

so monks engineered a ring
whose bottom arcs upheld the arms
and top quarter-circles buttressed the head,

perpendicular loads borne
by the curves carved thin enough to leave

four wedges of windy light
puncturing the tons of sober stone
still standing in the churchyard, fourteen feet high,

St. Martin's Cross, Iona,
its surface weathered away, its geometry solid.

Beggar's Lice

Sneaky mendicant weeds,
their little flat seedpods
would velcro themselves
to fur and socks and legs
as my dog and I romped
through grown-over fields,

bearing those hitchhikers
back home where I had to
unstick them one by one
until we were picked clean
of the wild green cooties
tenacious as hungry ticks,

begging (like us) the world
to take them anywhere else.

Loggerhead Hatchling

This tiny windup toy I could cup in one palm
can't stop turning in the wrong direction,

front flipperlets pulling it hard left or right,

away from the water glimmering straight ahead
and along the beach cooling as dusk expands

or back toward the nest it just dug out of, before

beginning a forty-yard crawl downslope from
the dune's repose to the whitecap Atlantic

along a smooth narrow runway graded for

dozens of turtles we hoped would soon begin
to escape the pit their mother dug months ago

before laying a hundred eggs she buried deep,

several feet under dry sand above high tide,
hidden from hungry raccoons and foxes and crabs

until the mini-loggerheads could push free into

our perilous twilight, onto the wide strand,
this first one veering off course again and again

though we gently steer it with the edge of a foot

or a blue-gloved hand back toward the ocean
it may not see with black peppercorn eyes

or hear with invisible ears gathering sound

into a head lifted to test late September wind:
finally it finds the spill of a retreating wave

and paddles gamely forward into shallow water

where breakers flip this scrap of living flotsam
once, twice, three times, a slapstick comedy

featuring one stoic figure battling the universe,

our plucky turtle righting and redirecting
until it can catch and ride the outgoing current,

a bite-sized being headed toward the horizon,

that urge to swim away profound as its mother's urge
to return to the very place where she was born

and clamber across the beach with strong flippers,

making her gravid way to the site from which
her hatchlings must try to make their own way,

leaving land for water as she left water for land,

out of their element for no longer than required,
each sandy half-ounce body leaving unmarked

the shore it navigates so poorly, against such odds.

Sunday Paper

We'd save change all week for one, a heavy handful
of quarters carried to the old Main Street drugstore
in our college town, lifting a *Times* or *Post* or *Globe*

from the gray stack by the door and swapping coins
for the big-city Sunday paper hauled back home
like a newborn in our arms, the inky musk of newsprint

pulled off the deafening presses just a few hours ago
mingling with coffee pot fumes as we spread out
all the sections across our thrift shop kitchen table:

I took sports or arts, she went for news or business,
we made slippery piles of the rest and started to read
slowly, like the idle rich, behind tall opened sheets

held before our faces, windows intently peered into,
now and then sharing a clever phrase or headline,
a peculiar detail from a wedding story or obituary,

the title of a new foreign movie we needed to see,
the name of a place that seemed worth traveling to,
though mostly the rustly uplifting and unfolding

was the soundtrack for each week's quietest morning,
those sentences typed and edited and made into pages
assembled and then delivered into our open hands,

leaving their mark on the fingertips we held them with,
with which we'd read each other later that holy day,
that smudgy touching sure proof of our worldliness.

The First

Yet again, I'm the first
to check out a new volume
of poetry, skinny book
whose skinny text is losing
its battle with white space,
and so the librarian must
glue an empty DATE DUE
slip to the half-title page
before stamping it in black
ink whose month day year
tells me how long I have

to be the first reader of
this version of the poems
filling my happy hands,
touching and turning them
till I reach the endpapers
and close the now-broken-in
book whose tender spine
I rub, and its tattooed skin,
maybe the last man to hold
a body that took somebody
so long to bring into being.

Dust to Dust

What edition of him
bought all these books,
lining their spines up
as if he would someday
reach for each volume
in alphabetical order
and open it to the light
and read from main title
to final choice syllable
then slip it precisely
back into its place, not

ignoring this library
until a cloudlet of dust
crowned every book,
narrow fuzzy shadows
settled on page edges,
gray inarticulate motes
his sneezing survivors
must wipe away before
trying to unload all
these written, printed,
bound, forgotten words?

The Death of Randall Jarrell

Chapel Hill, N.C., 14 October 1965

Was the unsteady man on the shoulder saluting,
or shielding his eyes from the blinding high beams?
As the passing car sideswiped him, or he the car,
the last thing he saw was his uplifted bare wrist.
Look how the crooked ghost of its stitches gleams.

The Roentgens

Wilhelm lifted Bertha's left hand
as he had on their wedding day

decades ago, squeezing and patting
and confirming its unseen bones

before placing it flat on the plate
and crossing the always chilly room

to release the new kind of radiation
he'd recently discovered by accident

late at night there in the laboratory
she hated, and resisted visiting,

though he'd finally convinced her
please to come, to sit, to be silent

for fifteen absolutely still minutes
while a stream of particles was directed

into and through her married hand,
making a photograph that would show

the human body for what it really was:
a skeleton whose pale fleshy cloud

melted away under bursts of waves
he called "x" rays because nobody knew

what their true nature was, or their effect
on the hidden solids brought to light

as the invisible revealed the invisible,
making transparencies of the opaque.

It was just before Christmas, 1895,
another cold snowy day in Würzburg.

Bertha wanted to go back upstairs
to their apartment, maybe put on gloves

and drink just one more demitasse
while reading under the lap blanket,

but she knew that Professor Roentgen
wanted her there, so there she was,

allowing him to take a slow exposure
that probed from wrist to fingertip:

it didn't hurt but it made her nervous,
like being scrutinized by Luther's God.

Wilhelm intended the photograph
to celebrate his scientific breakthrough

and encourage his always infirm wife,
her raised metacarpus flawless,

as if she were giving a cheerful greeting
to distinguished guests from afar.

Frau Roentgen's still-obscure bones
ached but she didn't dare shift or flex

until her husband said, "We're done."
The hand felt numb, despite hard rubbing.

When he proudly unveiled the image,
she gasped: it was a shadowy ghost,

a premonition that she'd die early,
an uplifted gesture that meant *farewell*,

goodbye fair skin I once thought was me,
death has dissolved my foolish tissues!

The darkest parts were her two rings,
which seemed to be floating too high

on the third fingerbone till she squinted
and saw they were as far down as possible,

surrounding and resting on mere flesh
ignored by those mysterious beams.

Bertha wanted to take both black circles
and throw them far out in the river

after her husband won the first Nobel Prize
for Physics, for his discovery of x-rays,

but she couldn't, they were famous now,
that hand was an international sensation,

strangers asked to see and touch it,
men bent for a kiss and lingered too long

as if they could sip the miracle radiation
it had absorbed for a stiff quarter-hour.

She wished that weird picture never existed.
It haunted many papers the week she died.

Frosted Windows in a Small-Town Presbyterian Church

No stained glass
for instruction or comfort,

just these plain whitened panes,
their blankness

a smothered glow
filling already numb mourners

with its anesthesia,
as if God's living breath pressed

against each window
from the cemetery just outside,

as if our own moist exhaled grief
fogged the cool glass,

leaving opaque pages
on which we wish we could write

her beloved name one last time
D   O   R   I   S

before the sun erases it,
before it becomes gray stone.

Thirst

A couple of blocks from the liquor store—
just long enough to leave its parking lot

and screw off the little cap while driving

then knock back a longed-for shot of spirits
and toss the emptied vial out the window,

throat already aglow with distilled warmth—

dozens of mini-bottles huddle in the ditch,
a glistening nest of thirst briefly relieved.

There, There

There, there, she'd console,
stroking my hair, rubbing my back
as I cried into her shoulder

and she repeated *There, there*,
a steady heartbeat
I could hear echo inside her body
and above my bowed head:

she said *There, there* the same
every time, the first word
stressed, rising,
its twin falling and fading away,

There, there   There, there
that doubled adverb
oddly comforting, a distancing
of whatever had upset me,

her *There, there* a calm Amen,
her soothing hands saying
I'm here   I'm here.

Sweet Chariot Car Wash

Slowest-motion tunnel
of most furious weather,
thundering sheets of rain
and low spinning clouds,
the air churned to lather:

we enter crusted with filth
but emerge immaculate,
a band of angels waiting
to wipe us dry, laughing,
snapping their soft towels.

Ovation

I stood on my stoop
and clapped her sneakers together
hard, a sharp report,
smacking right sole against left,
trying to shock the mud
from each overcomplicated tread,
spanking those expensive footprints
until clay flakes and plugs
ticked onto the boxwood's leaves
like a light filthy sleet
from the rubber craters and crannies
where they stuck weeks ago,
until her shoes were banged clean
though that didn't stop
my stiff-armed slow-motion applause
with her feet's emptied gloves,
slapping mate against mate
without missing a beat,
half wishing that hollow sound
echoing off the neighbors' houses
could call her back.

The Massage

After he tenderizes the tensed-up meat
that is my body, pale back and paler front—
kneading, gliding, rubbing, sudden tapping,
probing forgotten levels of my tissues
and stirring the sluggish circuit of the blood
with fingers whose deep pressure pushes me
past pleasure toward the verge of agony—
the therapist concludes our hour together
at the foot of the massage table, not moving
except for his hands holding my bare feet,
steadily gripping and then releasing them
by such gradual degrees that I can't tell
when his skin actually stops touching mine,
his warm oiled palms slowly pulling away
like a fade-out at the end of a film or song
so smooth I didn't notice it happening,
a mutual tapering-off and letting-go,
a welcome vanishing into black silence,
and though still flat on my back I feel as if
I'm standing, my feet rising from the ground
reluctant to bid them farewell yet lifting
their tingling soles gently up, that final layer
of cells in body and earth intermingling
so long it's hard to believe that I'm ascending.

Fats Waller

"Yeah, I yearn, sure I do, yeah!"
ad-libs Fats in the second verse of "S'posin,'"
one of a million throwaway jokes
he tossed off to mock some sappy lovesick lyric

with his popular portly clown act,
the eye-rolling, finger-wagging and ass-shaking
that hid how hard he'd had to work,
how he learned to play by slowing down piano rolls

and fingering the depressed keys,
how years at the Lincoln Theater's organ sharpened
his timing and sense of audience,
how he took lessons practicing Bach inventions

so he could play two strong hands
though his band said that he perfected his left
just so he could hold, in his right,
a glass brimful of gin. Yeah, he yearns, sure he does—

who doesn't?—for booze or food
or lingering kisses after a long night of music,
but his ear somehow transcribes
our common yearnings into joy. He said, "You got

to hang onto the melody
and never let it get boresome," and he never does:
no matter what sort of a song
Fats sits to play, he soon teases out its lively fun

and makes us part of his party,
ready to dance, and laugh, and have another drink
while the man in the beat-up derby
keeps loving that old upright with nimble fingers.

Michael McFee has taught poetry writing at the University of North Carolina-Chapel Hill since 1990. He is the author or editor of fifteen books: of his nine full-length poetry collections, the previous four—*That Was Oasis, Shinemaster, Earthly,* and *Colander*—were published by Carnegie Mellon. His second book of essays, *Appointed Rounds,* is forthcoming from Mercer University Press. A native of Asheville, North Carolina, he received the James Still Award for Writing about the Appalachian South from the Fellowship of Southern Writers in 2009.

Previous titles in the Carnegie Mellon Poetry Series

2007
Trick Pear, Suzanne Cleary
So I Will Till the Ground, Gregory Djanikian
Black Threads, Jeff Friedman
Drift and Pulse, Kathleen Halme
The Playhouse Near Dark, Elizabeth Holmes
On the Vanishing of Large Creatures, Susan Hutton
One Season Behind, Sarah Rosenblatt
Indeed I Was Pleased with the World, Mary Ruefle
The Situation, John Skoyles

2008
The Grace of Necessity, Samuel Green
After West, James Harms
Anticipate the Coming Reservoir, John Hoppenthaler
Convertible Night, Flurry of Stones, Dzvinia Orlowsky
Parable Hunter, Ricardo Pau-Llosa
The Book of Sleep, Eleanor Stanford

2009
Divine Margins, Peter Cooley
Cultural Studies, Kevin A. González
Dear Apocalypse, K. A. Hays
Warhol-o-rama, Peter Oresick
Cave of the Yellow Volkswagen, Maureen Seaton
Group Portrait from Hell, David Schloss
Birdwatching in Wartime, Jeffrey Thomson

2010
The Diminishing House, Nicky Beer
A World Remembered, T. Alan Broughton
Say Sand, Daniel Coudriet
Knock Knock, Heather Hartley
In the Land We Imagined Ourselves, Jonathan Johnson

Selected Early Poems: 1958-1983, Greg Kuzma
The Other Life: Selected Poems, Herbert Scott
Admission, Jerry Williams

2011
Having a Little Talk with Capital P Poetry, Jim Daniels
Oz, Nancy Eimers
Working in Flour, Jeff Friedman
Scorpio Rising: Selected Poems, Richard Katrovas
The Politics, Benjamin Paloff
Copperhead, Rachel Richardson

2012
Now Make an Altar, Amy Beeder
Still Some Cake, James Cummins
Comet Scar, James Harms
Early Creatures, Native Gods, K. A. Hays
That Was Oasis, Michael McFee
Blue Rust, Joseph Millar
Spitshine, Anne Marie Rooney
Civil Twilight, Margot Schilpp

2013
Oregon, Henry Carlile
Selvage, Donna Johnson
At the Autopsy of Vaslav Nijinsky, Bridget Lowe
Silvertone, Dzvinia Orlowsky
Fibonacci Batman: New & Selected Poems (1991-2011), Maureen Seaton
When We Were Cherished, Eve Shelnutt
The Fortunate Era, Arthur Smith
Birds of the Air, David Yezzi

2014
Alexandria, Jasmine Bailey
Night Bus to the Afterlife, Peter Cooley
Dear Gravity, Gregory Djanikian
Pretenders, Jeff Friedman

How I Went Red, Maggie Glover
All That Might Be Done, Samuel Green
The Wingless, Cecilia Llompart
Man, Ricardo Pau-Llosa

2015
The Octopus Game, Nicky Beer
The Voices, Michael Dennis Browne
Domestic Garden, John Hoppenthaler
We Mammals in Hospitable Times, Jynne Dilling Martin
And His Orchestra, Benjamin Paloff
Know Thyself, Joyce Peseroff
cadabra, Dan Rosenberg
The Long Haul, Vern Rutsala
Bartram's Garden, Eleanor Stanford

2016
Something Sinister, Hayan Charara
The Spokes of Venus, Rebecca Morgan Frank
Adult Swim, Heather Hartley
Swastika into Lotus, Richard Katrovas
The Nomenclature of Small Things, Lynn Pedersen
Hundred-Year Wave, Rachel Richardson
Where Are We in This Story, Sarah Rosenblatt
Inside Job, John Skoyles
Suddenly It's Evening: Selected Poems, John Skoyles

2017
Custody of the Eyes, Kimberly Burwick
Dream of the Gone-From City, Barbara Edelman
Windthrow, K. A. Hays
We Were Once Here, Michael McFee
Kingdom, Joseph Millar
The Histories, Jason Whitmarsh